Wrappings in Bespoke

By Sanjeev Sethi

Suddenly for Someone (1988, Atma Ram & Sons, Delhi)
Nine Summers Later (1997, Har-Anand, New Delhi)
This Summer and That Summer (2015, Bloomsbury, New Delhi)
Bleb (2021, Hybriddreich, Scotland)
Hesitancies (2021, CLASSIX, an imprint of Hawakal, New Delhi, and Kolkata)
Strokes of Solace (2022, CLASSIX, an imprint of Hawakal, New Delhi and Kolkata)

Wrappings in Bespoke

a book of poems

by

Sanjeev Sethi

First published 2022 by The Hedgehog Poetry Press

Published in the UK by
The Hedgehog Poetry Press
5, Coppack House
Churchill Avenue
Clevedon
BS21 6QW

www.hedgehogpress.co.uk

ISBN: 978-1-913499-28-0

9 8 7 6 5 4 3 2 1

A CIP Catalogue record for this book is available from the British Library.

For

Nana

&

Rohini

Contents

BIOG

Intertextuality of our ideas meet
on a spotless page to indite a
collaborative effort of strange
rhythms and sudden refrains.
Images and idioms speak our
accent. We coach ourselves to
ignore the commentators. In an
ecosystem of unequal genii, we
are happy to exist. To be is to
bloom. The rest is contextual.

SNATCH OF SCHOOLDAYS

A three-tonner transported us, shaking its way through
crosscuts and corridors of the cantonment. It was an
honourable way to hightail. As with all things army,
punctuality was the praxis. Kids weren't keyed into it.
On erring the local bus was my burrow. From my
headset, these were expeditions. I snaked my way
contiguous to the leadfoot, locus of the exit. There
were other straphangers. All rooted for him, laughed
at one-liners, supported his silliness. Influence of
being in the driver's seat came early.

LOSS AND OTHER LESSONS

(December, early seventies)

Ma was in hospital
with a heart condition.
We: sister and I
were at a friend's place.
Pa was at ** daddy's* funeral.

I remember, sister and me,
sitting on the parapet.
Sun was about to set.
That is when first essence
of loss filtered in.
This was not like losing
a pouch of picayunes.
This was big time loss.
As though someone had
punched my solar plexus.
The heart felt hard.
I wasn't even a teenager.

I remember her, my sister,
just about a teen, sitting
next to me. She seemed
much older, wiser, calmer.
I remember, looking at
her chocolate brown eyes,
looking at them for direction.
Her silence was palpable.
Finally she spoke:
"Don't feel bad. *Daddy* is with God."

Suddenly...
I was allayed of ache.
That sunset...
I learned my first big lesson:
Trust.

*Daddy: Mother's father a.k.a. *Nana*

TIDINGS

Efficiency of the memoriter ingress
allows you to come calling as easily
as another niggle of myself. Rain hits
upon me; in doing so, it robs me of
my right to say, No. This is Nature's
way, kowtow or kaput. Ocean, an
oriel away, gurgles and giggles to
share finespun specks of its latest
amour. I listen: it leavens.

RIGMAROLE

After the drill of social punctilios, when curtains are drawn, the blah
blah of bovarism lies peeled in those willing to eavesdrop on themselves.
Therapy of truth unveils its secrets: we know our lies better than all
the light there is. After a mortise level on laminate of life, it is meaningless
to tend to every kernel of truth. Attempts to amp this will end in ache.
The key is to find your centre. If there were a panopticon edge to one's script,
there wouldn't be need for prophets. To be famed for clerihews is meta.
Synesthesia bedrocks all impulses. What is the colour of your grief?
Pain isn't proprietary; join the party.

WISHES FOR A CHILD I NEVER HAD

I would want you not to be weak to the williwaw,
not to be vulnerable to whims of another. To be
girded with the resource to negotiate with niceties
of the nether. May you choose a domain that sways
in cadence to the music of your inscape.

An insight into the arts helps salve upheavals time thrusts upon us.
May the marrow in your bones be nourished by the vitamin
of wisdom. May the seed of compassion cultivate a garden
of goodness, enabling you to be a giver. May you be agile,
intuitive. May luck and its lustre broaden your borders.

TELEVISION

A regiment of railbirds
sterilized and sanctified
by social structures
dwell nightly as guests.
Their run or range never alters.
They never need any harrumphing.
Their recitals are true to their timbre.
In this gilly there are many gagsters
up to it in Grand Guignol.

On a quiet night
of which there are numerous,
I choose this babel of bellicose,
kind of corrida as sedative.

ALLOPATRY

There was a phase, longish period when I read,
I scrived but didn't put it in print. Tick-tock of
my pendulum was on a cerebrational mode.
Like a *bodhi* of sorts, I built a blindstory,
quieter than all the calm there is. College
friend, a bureaucrat, called. My apodictic
response was to share not show off. While
cutting off, his har-de-har translated as loser.

AVOIRDUPOIS

My mind drafted in mirror-writing
to help you decode me.
While sculling through choppiness
we adopted mismatched cant.
This took time to condense.

In a world packed with people
I miss metaphors of a tie-in.
In aloneness, I make do with myself,
speaking in tongues or through
cutouts of short-lived thrill.

Yes, the burden
of being me is heavy.

SELFDOM

Whirlwind of words ushers me to their crib.
As a sequel to alone time, chunks of my
conte appear. Relationships like piano wire
require skilful thrusts for tunable sounds to
breathe. Sourdough has its use. Connection
with self hastens confectionery of self-starting
gems: to hell with correctness and its charm.

CEREBRUM SPA

Ambry is stacked with shampoo,
toothpaste, and texturizing wax.
We rarely fail to pamper the frizzes
or follow up on our dental upkeep.
What about mental makeup? Are we
inclined towards iatric centres?
Streamlining phrenic routine, I realize
roster of positive influences.
The way is to breeze into hatchways
where bouncers nix the naysayers:
take every lemon lightly as when
checkmated at a convenience.

METAMORPHOSIS

In those eyes, oceans lose their way.
Music breaks into a new note: home
finds its hue. Roads stop competing.
Even loneliness finds something to
laugh about. Tonneau is tested. The
rumble seat holds empty bags. Proud
as pismires, we flourish in formicaries.
Even in transactional frameworks cer-
tain pacts are clued onto the unknown.
Chasing new curves results in rent. Is
transformation always positive?

RUBBER STAMP

The furuncle of those fifteen years lives
with me as no dermatologist is equipped
to dress it. I am told to travel to other
regions, but deadbolt positions fence me.
Some keys are of my making, others by
divine superintendence.

NAVIGATION

I never received emotional citizenship
in dominion of nanny days. Without
kedge of State sponsorship, I swam
in whirlpools. During my oceanic
phase, you and I: you as flotsam
I as me, stroked and stoked rough
weather. On menu of our meeting,
happiness was hazy. I elected for
other amusements in an island of
my making. Kelp, sea lion, and seal
are natant as caret is incised over me.
Muse, its mysteries are caretakers.

ULTIMA

Scars were wrapped in hyaline envelopes and
exchanged. Roundabout of rituals carried us.
So we thought? When crushed, the esoteric is
analgesic. We chided synastry and mismatched
dermatoglyphics. Sacerdotal engagement brought
us no ease. Wake of this windjammer ciphered its
synopsis.

MOVEMENT

Bookshelves remind me of the aloneness
of thought. In the stillness of their spines
lies the essence of experience beckoning
bibliophiles to process their perfections,
gleaned by grokking maze of milestones.

Solitude prods me to pylons. Known to
connect, they suspire for itinerant members
of the corvine to stop over or for deviations
in their dogleg. Every affiliation is emotional
travel. Close relationships are excursions.

BY THE WAY

Your eyewinker in my daybook requires no anatomizing
as your look-in is a day old. A lustrum ago, when spotted
eavesdropping or snooping for slips in my wallet or wardrobe,
you came at me with: what do you know what love is? I had no idea,
still don't. Silence seals it as I pucker my lips and blow you away.

EXPLORATIONS

Watchfully, divinity unwraps its bounties and blows.
Like a bystander at another's setback, I calm myself.
When legacy of loss is your fiefdom, fist pumps are
alien. Possibilities beckon me to the tarmac. Symbols
of the universe warn and warm me in strange ways
about wonted territories, some offshore.

IN TWOS

1

To breathe is to negotiate
with self, with superfluities.

2

Tailings turned into napalm. You lit it, and
wondered why I burned *that* easily?

3

Verisimilitude is ok.
Who wants all the truth?

4

I buzz a buddy: high-up on corporate hire, has he
heard his boss cut one? We laugh like we used to.

5

The sky roars, earth accepts:
those at lower end sharpen us.

6

Media maven: queue of those at your festival
indicates the qualia of your opinion.

7

Let yardsticks not be so severe; it's impossible to locate
subjects, faultlessness is akin to permanence here.

8

If prominence via slush pile is the aim
Heisman will be a part of your proof.

LEAVE-TAKING

You and I are no scholars of horology,
but time wraps in bespoke. Detritus
blocks our way, deterring us from
zooming into a xyst. We don't need
the descant of a dragoman. We know
it's clock out on a timepiece that refuses
to ticktock. When fresh, we lacked the grace
to smell the flowers. Rearranging an old
bouquet is no way to rev it up.

CONUNDRUM

The compositions on my corneas are in braille.
No need to tell me of the sinuosities between
us. Those engrams itch. I'm used to repeating
myself, like seeking shelter from charred ceilings.
Who do I execrate when one's soil is swidden?
Pathographies of our time guarantee I'm in a
good place. I wonder who creates this arrhythmia?
When face-to-face with the past, how does one
manage? I consume snifters: my way out of
messy corners. Déjàbrew is never a delight.

DILECTION

Was it love? I know not. You were a member
of my laterigrade moves. Incognito we become
ourselves like some of me: sans tags, I trudged.
It was a phase of intermezzos: petrichor never
was as redolent. Love danced, drank, ditched
with vigour as it is wont to. Other than that, my
mantel is empty. Memories are for monkeys.

ASAFETIDA

Investing emotions when other operating levers exist,
loving without the privilege of parenthood is an essay
in emptiness. In some eyes, I can see myself. I'm inured
to their throes. Come, let us camouflage grief in girdles
of guffaw. Let this be our chant.

You and I inhaled prescriptions scried by sources beyond
our breath. By then, my sight was misted by the smoke
of your sticky tune. As with passive smokers, we nip and
sometimes nurse. An opisthograph on love is not enough:
lived lives have other needs.

DISQUISITION

Searchlights within revealing the roost of my still small voice are on a glacis: nothing unusual, I'm getting on in years. Swizzle sticks are my way of keeping track in a bar. The nip between us glaces your eye, guttatim you defreeze. There is unrest between faultlines and fruition: believe me, I've detonated many. Yours is a phase. You, too, will curtsy. This is the charter of growing up.

DEUCE

Docked myself and waited. I remained uncut for years.
I exungulated. Tonsure artists worked on my visage.
When it was to meet, we met. I need a *Mary Norris*
to assist me with anxieties in choosing the en or em dash.
This restlessness is the mnemonic of my writing soufflé.

Repurposing one's scar for the in-between of another's
emotional and edifying sandwich is work of poet-chefs.
To brag about not being a humblebrag is being it. There
is need to bow to the other's belief: issues melt this way.
I wish I were born at 50, skipping the needle of nonage.

CONVERSATION WITH SELF

Your umbra is enough. I have installed
an imaginary portcullis on the edge
of my heart. I'm not ready for a close
up. I fear blackheads and untrimmed
hair in facial hollows. Authenticity
of this ache is a hierogram not drawn
in a hurry. We lived without a language,
loved without syntax. Our bodies spoke,
most of the time to ourselves or to those
hungers that seemed happy to have us.

Paradox and plurality are a part of our
processes. This unsureness is a blessing;
know-alls are for moral paladins or
the insane. My nights are as silent as
dramaturgy in books one does not
believe in. Insight isn't an accident.

JUNIOR

Her grandson, all of three, putters
around her, what is officially
her sleep time — tranquillizers
and all of that. She thinks it is love,
allows him this excess. For *putto*,
she is perhaps another plaything.

SOLUS

Physiognomy of childhood was cat's pyjamas
but constant changes in quick successions mottled
maps in my mind by implanting unseen wounds
metastasizing into unsigned and unspoken sequestration.

Aloneness by choice, I told myself or anyone
eager to apprehend. Excitations of amour?
Crosshatch of uncertainties dealt by my dearest.
Love is to abreact by anthologizing in ache.

PANORAMA

For the parched
semblance
of shower is enough.
Unruliness
of our union
is song
to saplessness.
Bias is built-in
the human chip.
This is an offshoot
of the temporal run.
It is not in the texture
of alluvial soil
to understand
ruth and rue
of the scorched.

PRACTITIONER

The physical form has never been my ally.
I exist in an aerosphere of my shaping.
The mind understands man-made sorrow
a razor-sharp within responds to God-given grief.

Wounds come easy, like the tales I tell myself.
When silence sets in, I flow and flower.
It has taken me years to meet with vocabulary
capable of concealing my wales. But to no avail.

Camouflage is now a shift. The chiffonier is stocked.
A fresh drench of rancid rain fells me with her dole.
To a more robust combination, this may have been less heartfelt.
I am OK. A seasoned hack, I have the advantage of age.

IN EUROPE

The flight attendant was efficient and effective.
I asked if work interfered with her family life.
"I have no family, just a cluster of cats." She responded.

I forgot to ask, in her absence,
who took care of her clowder.

RICOCHET

Unlike broken goods, broken people need pampering.
For one, they believe they have been shortchanged.
In this warren, I endearingly call home, doors away
from mine, a fellow as old as I said so long.

Following noon cops found him on the davenport.
His act has me unaffected. Am I doing this number
as his narrative mirrors mine? Well, almost. I'm alive.

MARIONETTE

In the statuary of my branular orb, your figurine shines the sharpest.
When fate conspires to have us face to face, you bring to nought
the herringbone fabric I primp your mannequin with. I like the layers
I pad you with: you're you, plus my decoupage. This suits our setting.
The dominion of physical distance invigorates our weal with you
chirking best inside me, heedful of my heart as your homestead.

GETUP

Every time she shines in a sari
I inquire, how many? The query
gladdens her at many levels: *she
has things to hide.* Like an able
and acute hoarder she turns mealy-
mouthed, tightens her eyes, and
in silken drawl reviews with me
menu of the day.

*SACRAMENT

Trying to reconcile with the recondite
lines of your life results in asphyxiation.
You are oblivious of me, my *bacha*,
oblivious of my anxieties, our ado.

While we are numbed by this numinous play,
it's you who is sniggering in stealth.
Perhaps you know the truths of your travel.
We must accept you as you are.
That is the ukase of grace.

In acceptance is our arrival
to embrace corrective anthems.
That is our need. You're complete
with your cackle, my child.

*For a friend's little girl,
rare in her quiet way.*

DEBATE

finding
righteousness
in polarity
each perspective
an outcome
of optics
a by-product
of its tendentiousness
your correctness
is creation
of your cosmos
every verdict
a version
of its colophon

SECRETS

Sublingual secrets are minacious:
of them glissading
as scuttlebutt is imminent.
Never dread the locus
of your confidentialness.
Be on the qui vive for palsy-walsy
carriers of the gravamen.
It's always the squealer's failing,
specious to censure provocateurs.

DRUTHERS

Memories without an outlet are a mass of uncoded messages
lazing around in maziness of the mind, like an unused
clutch of wires in a mesh of sheepshanks elsewhere.
The prodrome was the smile and the ardour in your canthus.
Anaesthetized by the notion of togetherness, in my stupor
I vocalized a vision. Do I blame the stupor? Or the anaesthetist?
I have chosen to exculpate myself. That is the good part
about clearing wreckage; we choose what stokes us.

MEGRIMS

I am peeved when poems look like poems. It is the same
with people. Treacle gets to me. I am good with gruffness
if that heart has a beat. It is discomforting to decode cyphers
in spaces of peradventure. Comfort lies in contextual certitudes.
I turn to switch words when my circuit needs decluttering.
In this haze, curlicues of desire shine to your capriciousness.
Time for emotional éboulement is over. The road is ready.

TUNEFUL

When *legit* poets and their legally wedded
wives ask, "What do you *actually* do?" I
sense their agita. I understand when others
segue this with pleasantries and puff. At my
age, I catch on, some I choose not to. This
helps with the horizons.

ACKNOWLEDGEMENTS

Grateful Acknowledgements to the following journal
where some of the poems were first published (in no
particular order).

*London Grip, Ink, Sweat and Tears, Sentinel Literary Quarterly,
Amaryllis Poetry, The Open Mouse, Postcolonial Text, Otoliths,
Bluepepper, Eunoia Review, Lemon Hound, Hamilton Stone Review,
Off the Coast, Linden Avenue Literary Journal, Red Wolf Journal, Mad
Swirl, Red Fez, Spirit Fire Review, Section 8 Magazine, Futures Trading,
Revolution John, Pyrokinection, Indefinite Space, Right Hand Pointing,
Poetrymagazine.com, Chronogram, The Jawline Review, Synesthesia
Literary Journal, Yellow Mama, Dime Show Review, Olentangy Review,
Literary Orphans, Muse India,* and *Coldnoon.*

PRAISE FOR SANJEEV SETHI

"Sanjeev Sethi's poems are notable for conciseness, for their clarity. Observations, when they are made, are witty, succinct, and relevant. Words are crucial. With them, they carry symbolism, wizardry, enchantment, magic. The more I read him, the more I find myself sharing in the author's love of and relish for words in all their subtleties and guises."

Mandy Pannett, Sentinel Literary Quarterly, UK

"Sanjeev Sethi uses his personal condition to illustrate our human condition. The message throughout encourages me to overcome my own hesitancies to engage, take risks, embrace failure as the impetus to growth – and lighten up a little, laugh at myself a little, have faith!"

MH Clay, Mad Swirl, USA

"Sharp as bullets and soft as silk, they touch each reader variously. Wordsmith, raconteur, witness to global change, Sanjeev Sethi writes with confident innovations."

Malashri Lal, Outlook Magazine, India